D080000062

INFLUENCING FOR OPPORTUNITY

Identify and maximize ways to influence

CATHERINE MATTISKE

TPC - The Performance Company Pty Ltd
PO Box 639
Rozelle NSW 2039
Sydney, Australia

ACN 077 455 273
email: info@tpc.net.au
Website: www.tpc.net.au

National Library of Australia
Cataloguing-in-Publication data

Mattiske, Catherine
Influencing for Opportunity: Identify and Maximize Ways to Influence

ISBN 978-1-921547-10-2

1. Occupational training   2. Learning   I. Title

370.113

Printed in USA

Distributed by TPC - The Performance Company - www.tpc.net.au
For further information contact TPC - The Performance Company, Sydney Australia on +61 9555 1953 or
TPC - The Performance Company, California on +1 818-227-5052, or email info@tpc.net.au

HELLO.

Welcome to the Learning Short-take® process!

This Learning Short-take® is a bite sized learning package that aims to improve your skills and provide you with an opportunity for personal and professional development to achieve success in your role.

This Learning Short-take® combines self study with workplace activities in a unique learning system to keep you motivated and energized. So let's get started!

Step 1:
What's inside?

- Learning Short-take® Participant Guide. This section contains all of the learning content and will guide you through the learning process.
- Learning Activities. You will be prompted to complete these as you read through the Participant Guide.
- Learning Journal. This is a summary of your key learnings. Update it when prompted.
- Skill Development Action Plan. Learning is about taking action. This is your action plan where you'll plan how you will implement your learning.

Step 2:
Complete the Learning Short-take®

- Learning Short-takes® are best completed in a quiet environment that is free of distractions.
- Schedule time in your calendar to complete the Learning Short-take® and prioritize this time as an investment in your own professional development.
- Depending on the title, most participants complete the Learning Short-take® from 90 minutes to 2.5 hours.

Step 3:
Meet with your Manager/Coach

- Schedule a 30 minute meeting with your Manager or Coach.
- At this meeting share your completed Activities, Learning Journal and Skill Development Action Plan.
- Most importantly, discuss and agree on how you will implement your learning in your role.

Welcome

Influencing for Opportunity
Identify and Maximize Ways to Influence

Influencing for Opportunity combines self-study with realistic workplace activities to provide you with the key skills and techniques to influence those around you. You will learn the theory of influence, influence principles and strategies, as well as how to plan and prepare for important opportunities to influence. As a result, you should achieve greater results in your organization, work more productively and effectively in a team environment, and develop stronger working relationships with co-workers, suppliers and customers.

The ability to influence others is critical in today's competitive business environment. Being highly skilled in influence enables you to build the relationships you need to get results inside or outside the organization. Employees and managers alike cannot assume they have power over others - they must earn it through influence. Being an influential person is a skill that can be learned and practiced. **Influencing for Opportunity** will help you succeed in the modern corporate environment by increasing your ability to influence others.

Influencing for Opportunity includes a Job Aid and learning support tool, **'6 Rules of Influence'**, provided to you as a free download.

Now let's get started!

> "To listen well is as powerful a means of influence as to talk well and is as essential to all true conversation."
>
> Ancient Proverb

"It is easier to influence strong than weak characters in life. "

Margot Asquith

Section 1

PARTICIPANT GUIDE

Start here

What's in this Participant Guide

"I seek the serenity to accept what I cannot change; the courage to change what I can; and the wisdom to know the difference."

Author unknown

Table of Contents

How to Complete your Learning Short-take®

1. **Reflect on your skills and abilities** in influencing others, and how you use this information to improve effectiveness in your role.

2. **Complete the Activities as directed.**

3. **Highlight specific skill areas** that you believe you could develop more. Add these to the Learning Journal as you proceed through the Learning Short-take®.

4. When you have completed this Learning Short-take® **meet with your Manager/Coach**. In this meeting, you will jointly establish a personal Skill Development Action Plan.

5. **Subject to your coach's final review** and assessment, you will either sign off the module, or undertake further skill development as appropriate.

"No star ever rose or set without influence somewhere."

Lord Edward Robert Bulwer Lytton,
"Owen Meredith", Lucile
(pt. II, canto VI)

Activity Checklist

"A teacher affects eternity; he can never tell where his influence stops. "

Henry Brooks Adams

During this Learning Short-take® you will be prompted to complete the following activities:

Learning Objectives

By the end of this Learning Short-take® you should be able to:

- Identify patterns of influence.

- Evaluate how you currently use influence behaviors and identify areas for development.

- Develop influence behaviors for greater personal and business success.

- Establish clear and powerful influence goals.

- Increase influence to overcome resistance.

- Describe how to ask for and receive support.

- Design an approach for formal and informal influence situations; apply the approach to a real-life situation.

- Create a Skill Development Action Plan.

"You can exert no influence if you are not susceptible to influence."

Carl Jung

Let's Get Started

"There are, then, these three means of effecting persuasion. The man who is to be in command of them must, it is clear, be able (1) to reason logically, (2) to understand human character and goodness in their various forms, and (3) to understand the emotions - that is, to name them and describe them, to know their causes and the way in which they are excited."

Aristotle, Rhetoric I, ch. 2)

Influence is a rapidly expanding field devoted to discovering the principles that determine beliefs, create attitudes, and move people to agreement and action. In other words, influence examines the process that causes humans to *change*.

When influence is used correctly, it efficiently moves people in positive directions. Those who wish to create and sustain positive change in others need to understand how the influence process works.

This Learning Short-take® combines self-study with workplace activities to provide you with the key skills to influence others ethically. You will learn how to influence individuals and groups to reach successful outcomes. You will undertake a series of activities that will assist you in developing your influencing skills. The Learning Short-take® is designed for completion in approximately 90 minutes.

8

FUNDAMENTALS
OF INFLUENCE

Part 1

The Ability to Influence

1

Social influence is when the actions or thoughts of individual(s) are changed by other individual(s).

Social science is committed to expanding the knowledge of how people are persuaded and why they are compliant with requests from others. The science of Social Influence has discovered how to increase your likelihood of hearing "yes," sometimes as much as 300% or 400%, by merely adding a word or phrase, or changing the sequence of your request.

A knowledge of influence can help you when you need to move someone to adopt a new attitude, belief, or action. It can also help you resist the influence attempts of others. This Learning Short-take® is designed to help you become a more persuasive person, but also to help you better recognize the influence attempts of others.

The Science of Social Influence - 384 to Current

Aristotle
384—322 ,
Greek philosopher

Since Aristotle recorded his principles of persuasion in Rhetoric, humans have attempted to define and refine the principles of successful influence.

Persuasion has been studied as an art for most of human history. Aristotle said that "Rhetoric is the art of discovering, in a particular case, the available means of persuasion."

The comparatively young science of social influence, however, can trace its roots to the second world war, when a social psychologist named Carl Hovland was contracted by the U.S. Armed Forces to bolster the morale of soldiers. President Roosevelt was concerned that Americans would lose the will to fight after winning victory in Europe.

It was Hovland's job to motivate soldiers to continue fighting against Japan. Since World War II, social influence has become a vastly expanding field of study devoted to discovering the principles that determine our beliefs, create our attitudes, and move us to action.

Persuasion NOT Manipulation

Persuasion

Persuasion is a form of influence. It is the process of guiding people toward the adoption of an idea, attitude, or action by rational and symbolic (though not only logical) means. It is a problem-solving strategy, and relies on "appeals" rather than force. Persuasion is meant to benefit all parties.

Manipulation

In a psychological context, manipulation means to influence a person or a group of people in such a way that the manipulator tries to get what he or she wants, or makes a person believe something in a calculating, indirect and somewhat dishonest way. A manipulator may do any or all of the following:

- use arguments that the manipulator does not believe in
- use false reasoning
- withhold or distort relevant information,
- provide false information (disinformation)
- "Play" on the emotions (fear, hope, love...) of the person.

Three Components of Social Influence

There are 3 components of social influence:

Conformity

A type of social influence in which individuals change their attitudes or behavior in order to adhere to existing social norms.

Compliance

A form of social influence involving direct request from one person to another.

Obedience

A form of social influence in which one person obeys direct orders from another to perform some action(s).

Complete Activity # 1
Initial Skills Assessment

Activity 1: Initial Skills Assessment

Understanding the key elements of influencing others is critical to improving business and personal success. This assessment covers the core skills in influence.

Rate yourself on each of the techniques.

7 is competent and confident, little need for improvement

4 is average, needs improvement

1 is uncomfortable, major need for improvement

- Note specific areas of improvement related to each skill that you would like to develop. Be sure to include your **reasons** for your rating in each skill, as this reasoning will be a key part of the initial goal setting session with your coach.

- Start thinking about a personal development plan and identify two things you could do to improve your skills in this area and write them in the space provided.

I...	Rating	Reasoning
1. know how my colleagues and manager assess my work performance.	1 2 3 4 5 6 7	
2. am seen as a top performer.	1 2 3 4 5 6 7	
3. am a 'go-to' person.	1 2 3 4 5 6 7	
4. am the person people turn to when a task has a high degree of difficulty.	1 2 3 4 5 6 7	
5. am confident people view me as ethical.	1 2 3 4 5 6 7	
6. am known for honesty and openness.	1 2 3 4 5 6 7	
7. know that others are clear on what I stand for.	1 2 3 4 5 6 7	
8. walk my talk (i.e. I am consistent in what I say I will do with what I do).	1 2 3 4 5 6 7	
9. am seen by others as empathetic.	1 2 3 4 5 6 7	

Please turn over to complete

Activity 1: Continued

I...	Rating	Reasoning
10. am seen by others to have their best interests at heart.	1 2 3 4 5 6 7	
11. am known as good listener and one who doesn't jump to conclusions before hearing people out.	1 2 3 4 5 6 7	
12. am cool under pressure.	1 2 3 4 5 6 7	
13. am effective and professional when passions are high and/or deadlines are tight.	1 2 3 4 5 6 7	
14. am known as generous with my time and ideas, even in areas outside my immediate work duties.	1 2 3 4 5 6 7	
15. have people comfortably confiding in me or asking me to coach or mentor them.	1 2 3 4 5 6 7	
16. feel better about the work when I'm on the team.	1 2 3 4 5 6 7	

If an individual is seen as lacking in any one area: expertise, integrity or empathy, that person's influence is significantly diminished. Those qualities in combination grow and sustain your influence. Reflect on your answers and consider how to improve your influence.

Personal development plan ideas:

1

2

Now update your Learning Journal (page 61)

INFLUENCE:
A CHOICE

Part 2

Control vs. Influence

One of the keys to changing our world for the better, and relieving ourselves from a great deal of worry and stress, is in recognizing those things that we can effect. We cannot control everything in our lives. Some things, like our own behavior and reactions to the things that happen to us, are completely under our control. Other things, like our customers, are not completely under our control, but we do have a lot of influence over them. Finally, there are things that are completely outside of our influence. The actions of a foreign government, the behavior of a movie star, the price of gasoline are all things that most of us have no influence over.

Some things we have no real control over, and others we can do something about. In the model by Stephen Covey these things are separated into 'concern' and 'influence'. By determining which of these two circles is the focus of most of our time and energy, we can discover much about the degree of our proactivity.

Everyone has much to be concerned about. Health, family, work issues, community concerns and issues concerning society as a whole. These things make up our Circle of Concern.

Within the Circle of Concern, there are issues about which we have no real control and others that we can do something about. By identifying the concerns about which we can do something, we can proactively do something to influence a positive outcome. These concerns are moved from the Circle of Concern and put into the Circle of Influence.

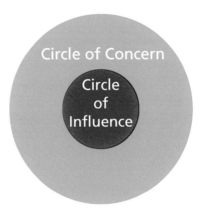

This proactive approach allows us to mentally 'park' issues over which we have not control, for now or forever. Doing this allows us to proactively focus on **what we can do**. When we accept the things that we can't immediately control, it frees us to focus on the things we can do something about.

The nature of this approach is positive, therefore over time, the Circle of Influence increases. By adopting this approach, we shift our focus to reduce the amount of time worrying, being unhappy and distressed, to building encouragement and hope as we address and resolve issues in the Circle of Influence.

The first step in implementing this model is to identify our concerns. Then, separate them into the Circle of Concern (i.e. concerns that can be 'parked'), and the Circle of Influence.

Then, for an initial period of time, say, 30 days, focus on the Circle of Influence. Testing this principle of proactivity for 30 days by consciously working in the Circle of Influence, means making small commitments daily, ensuring the process is without judgment (i.e. if it goes astray that's OK, just get back on track!), and without being a critic.

It's about having the courage not be part of the problem, but rather influence the solution.

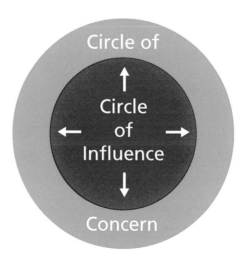

Now update your Learning Journal (page 61)

18

NATURALLY OCCURRING INFLUENCE PATTERNS

Part 3

Agents of Influence

Dr. Cialdini, a social psychologist who has studied natural influence in society, distinguishes agents of influence of three types: Bunglers, Smugglers, and Sleuths.

The Bungler is the individual who doesn't understand how to use the most powerful principles of influence and, consequently, fumbles away opportunities for beneficial change.

The Smuggler is the person who understands these principles of influence perfectly well, but who uses them dishonestly producing gain that is one-sided and temporary. This behavior aligns to the definition of manipulation.

The Sleuth, on the other hand, uncovers the powerful principles that naturally reside in the influence situation and brings them to the surface to the long-term advantage of both parties.

Complete Activity # 2
Agents of Influence

Activity 2: Agents of Influence

Reflect on both professional and personal events in your life. Recall situations in as much detail as you can.

1

In your Professional / Business life

	What happened?	How did you feel?	What was the long term result?
The Bungler: When have you Bungled away an opportunity that later you realized could have been to your benefit?			
The Smuggler: When have you had someone be dishonest with you in order to manipulate you into doing something?			
The Sleuth: When have you uncovered possible ways to influence a situation in order to get a win/win outcome (i.e. benefit for both parties).			

In your Personal life
(Home, family, community, friends)

	What happened?	How did you feel?	What was the long term result?
The Bungler: When have you Bungled away an opportunity that later you realized could have been to your benefit?			
The Smuggler: When have you had someone be dishonest with you in order to manipulate you into doing something?			
The Sleuth: When have you uncovered possible ways to influence a situation in order to get a win/win outcome (i.e. benefit for both parties).			

Now update your Learning Journal (page 61)

6 Rules of Influence

1 - Rule of Reciprocity

According to sociologists, one of the most widespread and basic norms of human culture is embodied in the rule of reciprocity. The rule requires that one person tries to repay, in kind, what another person has provided.

By obligating the recipient of an act to repay in the future, the rule for reciprocity allows one person to give something, with confidence that it will be repaid at some future time.

Future Obligation

This sense of future obligation within the rule makes possible the development of various kinds of continuing relationships, transactions, and exchanges that are beneficial to the society.

Consequently, all members of the society are trained from childhood to abide by the rule or suffer serious social disapproval.

Giving before asking for something in return

The decision to comply with another's request is frequently influenced by the reciprocity rule. One favorite and profitable tactic is to give something to another before asking for a return favor.

The Power of Reciprocity

The exploitability of this tactic is due to three characteristics of the rule for reciprocation:

- the rule is extremely powerful, often overwhelming the influence of other factors that normally determine compliance with a request

- the rule applies even to uninvited first favors, thereby reducing our ability to decide whom we wish to owe and putting the choice in the hands of others

- the rule can spur unequal exchanges; to be rid of the uncomfortable feeling of indebtedness, an individual will often agree to a request for a substantially larger favor than the one he or she received.

2 - Commitment and Consistency

People have a desire to look consistent within their words, beliefs, attitudes and deeds. This tendency is fed from three sources:

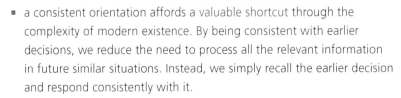

- good personal consistency is highly valued by society

- consistent conduct provides a beneficial approach to daily life

- a consistent orientation affords a valuable shortcut through the complexity of modern existence. By being consistent with earlier decisions, we reduce the need to process all the relevant information in future similar situations. Instead, we simply recall the earlier decision and respond consistently with it.

Complete Activity # 3
Influence Rules in Action

Activity 3: Influence Rules in Action

Reflect on the first two rules of social influence: Reciprocity, and Commitment and Consistency. Complete the following table.

	Reciprocity	Commitment and Consistency
In your own words define each rule		
What are the three key learnings of each rule?	1 2 3	1 2 3
In business, why does this rule matter to me?		
In my personal life, why does this rule matter to me?		
Why does this rule matter to others that I work with - colleagues, customers, suppliers etc		
Why does this rule matter to my organization?		

Now update your Learning Journal (page 61)

3 - Social Proof

One means we use to determine what is correct is to find out what other people think is correct.

We view behavior as more correct in a given situation to the degree that we see others performing it.

The principle of social proof can be used to stimulate a person's compliance with a request by informing the person that many other individuals (the more, the better, the more "famous" the better) are or have been complying with it.

As with the other "weapons of influence," social proof is a shortcut that usually works well for us: if we conform to the behavior we see around us, we are less likely to make a social faux pas.

When we do not know how to behave, we copy other people. They act as an information source for how to behave, and we assume they know what they are doing. Given that we care a great deal about what others think about us, this provides a safe course of action - at the very least, they cannot criticize us for our actions. The tendency for people to "follow suit" trades on the bandwagon fallacy.

Example of "following suit":

Experiments have found that the use of recorded laughter causes an audience to laugh longer and more often when humorous material is presented and to rate the material as funnier.

Private acceptance occurs when we genuinely believe the other person is right. This can lead to permanent changes in beliefs, values and behaviors.

Public compliance occurs when we copy others because we fear ridicule or rejection if we behave otherwise.

Social Proof occurs most often when:

- The situation is ambiguous. We have choices but do not know which to select.

- There is a crisis. We have no time to think and experiment. A decision is required now!

- Others are experts. If we accept the authority of others, they must know better than us.

- Social proof is most influential under two conditions: Liking and Authority.

4 - Liking

People prefer to say yes to individuals they know and like. This simple rule enables us to learn about factors that influence the liking process by examining which factors compliance professionals emphasize to increase their overall attractiveness and their consequent effectiveness.

Compliance practitioners regularly use several such factors.

- One feature of a person that influences people is physical attractiveness. Although it has long been suspected that physical beauty provides an advantage in social interaction, research indicates that the advantage may be greater than supposed. Physical attractiveness seems to engender a "halo" effect that extends to favorable impressions of other traits such as talent, kindness, and intelligence. As a result, attractive people are more persuasive both in terms of getting what they request and in changing others' attitudes.

- A second factor that influences liking and compliance is similarity. We like people who are like us and are more willing to say yes to their requests, often in an unthinking manner.

27

- Another factor that produces liking is praise; although they can sometimes backfire when crudely transparent, compliments generally enhance liking, and thus, compliance. Increased familiarity through repeated contact with a person or thing is yet another factor that normally facilitates liking. But this relationship holds true principally when the contact takes place under positive rather than negative circumstances.

- One positive circumstance that works especially well is mutual and successful cooperation.
- The final factor linked to liking is mere association. By connecting themselves or their products with positive things, The Influence Sleuths frequently seek to share in the positive experience through the process of association.

Peer Pressure - Aim: Liking

In the case of peer pressure, a person might be forced into doing something he/she might not like but is "necessary" to upkeep the positive relationship with the other party.

5 - Authority

We can see evidence of a strong pressure in our society for compliance with the requests of an authority. Our practice to obey legitimate authorities comes from socialization practices designed to instill in society the perception that such obedience constitutes correct conduct.

When reacting to authority in an automatic fashion, there is a tendency to do so in response to the mere symbols of authority rather than to its substance.

Three kinds of symbols that have been shown by research to be effective in this regard are:

- Titles
- Clothing
- Automobiles
- Other trappings of wealth.

In separate studies investigating the influence of these symbols, individuals possessing one or another of them (and no other legitimizing credentials) were accorded more deference or obedience by those they encountered. Moreover, in each instance, those individuals who deferred or obeyed, underestimated the effect of authority pressures on their behaviors.

Questioning Authority

It is possible to defend ourselves against the detrimental effects of authority influence by asking two questions:

- Is this authority truly an expert?
  The first question directs our attention away from symbols and toward evidence for authority status.
- How truthful can we expect this expert to be here?
  The second advises us to consider not just the expert's knowledge in the situation but also his or her trustworthiness. With regard to this second consideration, we should be alert to the trust-enhancing tactic in which a communicator first provides some mildly negative information about him - or herself.

Through this strategy the person creates a perception of honesty that makes all subsequent information seem even more credible to observers.

Complete Activity # 4
Drivers of Social Proof: Liking and Authority

Activity 4: Drivers of Social Proof: Liking and Authority

Reflect on three rules of Social Influence: Social Proof, Liking and Authority.
Complete the diagram below.

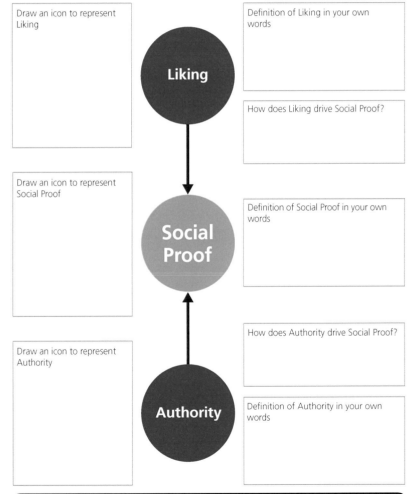

Draw an icon to represent Liking

Definition of Liking in your own words

How does Liking drive Social Proof?

Liking

Draw an icon to represent Social Proof

Social Proof

Definition of Social Proof in your own words

Draw an icon to represent Authority

How does Authority drive Social Proof?

Authority

Definition of Authority in your own words

Now update your Learning Journal (page 61)

6 - Scarcity

According to the scarcity principle, people assign more value to opportunities when they are less available.

The use of this principle for profit can be seen in such compliance techniques as the "limited number" and "deadline" tactics, wherein practitioners try to convince us that access to what they are offering is restricted by amount or time.

The scarcity principle holds true for two reasons:

- because things that are difficult to attain are typically more valuable, the availability of an item or experience can serve as a cue to its quality.

- as things become less accessible, we lose freedoms. According to psychological reactance theory, we respond to the loss of freedoms by wanting to have them (along with the goods and services connected to them) more than before.

Optimum Conditions for Scarcity

The scarcity principle is most likely to hold true under two optimizing conditions:

- Scarce items are heightened in value when they are newly scarce (we value those things that have become recently restricted more than those that were restricted all along). For example the hottest concert tickets, the newest restaurant in town, or the latest fashion item.

- We are most attracted to scarce resources when we compete with others for them. For example, an auction, a reward at work, the opening sale at an exclusive department store.

It is difficult to steel ourselves cognitively against scarcity pressures because they have an emotion-arousing quality that makes thinking difficult. Once alerted, we can take steps to calm the arousal and assess the merits of the opportunity in terms of why we want it.

Complete Activity # 5
6 Rules of Influence

Activity 5: 6 Rules of Influence

1

For each statement choose the best answer.

1. People are more likely be persuaded by you if:
   - a) they feel a sense of obligation to you
   - b) if you have provided a 'first favour'
   - c) they are moderately concerned about the topic
   - d) both a & b

2. If you're attempting to sell a customer an item from your company's lineup of three models (the 'economy,' the 'midrange,' and the 'luxury' model), research has demonstrated you will obtain higher sales figures by:
   - a) starting at the bottom and moving up the line
   - b) starting at the top and moving down the line
   - c) starting at the middle and then allowing customers to 'own the decision' by moving up or down the line themselves

3. Years of tracking political elections have revealed that the single most reliable predictor of who will win an election is the candidate who:
   - a) is the most physically attractive
   - b) produces the greatest number of negative or 'attack' ads against his or her opponent
   - c) has the most active and committed volunteer base
   - d) spends the most time focusing on the issues

4. Research has shown the general relationship between self-esteem and the ability to be persuaded to be:
   - a) people with low self-esteem are the most persuadable
   - b) people with average self-esteem are the most persuadable
   - c) people with high self-esteem are the most persuadable

5. Imagine you are the campaign manager of a political candidate who has recently lost the public's trust. Now imagine that the candidate wants to rebuild his or her reputation through profiling themselves as a tough crime-fighter. Of the following choices, which represents the best way for your candidate to start his next ad?
   - a) 'My opponent has not gone far enough in fighting crime . . .'
   - b) 'Many have supported my ability and willingness to fight crime . . .'
   - c) 'Although my opponent has a good record of fighting crime, . . .'

6. Imagine you are a financial advisor, and you believe that a young client of yours is invested too conservatively. In order to persuade him or her to invest in riskier, high-return investments, you should concentrate on describing:
   - a) how others like her have made similar mistakes
   - b) what she stands to gain if she invests in riskier options
   - c) how others like her have made significant gains in high-return investments

Activity 5: Continued

7. Research has demonstrated that jurors are most persuaded by:
   - a) an expert witness who uses easy-to-understand terms
   - b) an expert witness who speaks in incomprehensible language
   - c) a witness who speaks with conviction

8. When faced with a choice of movies, sporting events, theatre productions or restaurants, people are most likely to choose to go to the one:
   - a) based on the size of the event and the availability of tickets
   - b) based on popularity, written reviews, and because a personal friend has recommended it
   - c) based on the star performer and popularity of the event

9. Imagine you are a consultant trying to influence a client (internal client or external client) to do business. The client asks to meet with you. To increase your influence you should:
   - a) give the client one or two possible dates/times
   - b) give the client as many possible appointment times in the next week
   - c) tell the client you'll see him or her in 45 minutes
   - d) ask the client for a date/time that suits them, as your calendar is completely open
   - e) meet over the phone as quickly as possible and avoid the face-to-face meeting

10. Imagine you are conducting a performance review for an underperforming staff member. In order to maximize the staff member correcting their behavior, at the end of the meeting you should:
    - a) end on a cheery note
    - b) offer support
    - c) talk generally about their family and social life
    - d) have the staff member say exactly what actions he or she wants to take within an agreed timeline

11. In a presentation, which of the following statements would you not choose:
    - a) I am not the expert in this area and would welcome your input
    - b) Since receiving this project last month I have consulted with industry leaders, our business partners and undertaken competitive research regarding the implementation of the proposed process
    - c) Like you, we are all challenged by change
    - d) Today, as we have a brief time together, I have invited John Bellmore, the widely recognized expert in…
    - e) Thank you for sending me your feedback on the project to date. I have compiled your comments and suggestions and formulated a revised project plan. Today, I am seeking your commitment to this plan

12. The six most fundamental principles of influence to be discovered by social psychological research are:
    - a) enthusiasm, pleasantness, dissonance, memory, attention & positive associations
    - b) attending, pacing, hypnosis, mirroring, archetypes & subliminal persuasion
    - c) commitment/consistency, authority, reciprocity, liking, social proof & scarcity

1

Check your Answers!

Activity #5 - 6 Rules of Influence

For each statement choose the best answer.

1. People are more likely be persuaded by you if:
   d) Both a & b

2. If you're attempting to sell a customer an item from your company's lineup of three models (the "economy," the "midrange," and the "luxury" model), research has demonstrated you will obtain higher sales figures by:

   b) starting at the top and moving down the line

3. Years of tracking political elections have revealed that the single most reliable predictor of who will win an election is the candidate who:
   a) is the most physically attractive

4. Research has shown the general relationship between self-esteem and the ability to be persuaded to be:
   b) people with average self-esteem are the most persuadable

5. Imagine you are the campaign manager of a political candidate who has recently lost the public's trust. Now imagine that the candidate wants to rebuild his or her reputation through profiling themselves as a tough crime-fighter. Of the following choices, which represents the best way for your candidate to start his next ad?
   c) "Although my opponent has a good record of fighting crime..."

6. Imagine you are a financial advisor, and you believe that a young client of yours is invested too conservatively. In order to persuade him or her to invest in riskier, high-return investments, you should concentrate on describing:
   c) how others like her have made significant gains in high-return investments

7. Research has demonstrated that jurors are most persuaded by:
    b) an expert witness who speaks in incomprehensible language

8. When faced with a choice of movies, sporting events, theatre productions or restaurants, people are most likely to choose to go to the one
    b) based on popularity, written reviews, and because a personal friend has recommended it

9. Imagine you are a consultant trying to influence a client (internal client or external client) to do business. The client asks to meet with you. To increase your influence you should
    a) give the client one or two possible dates/times

10. Imagine you are conducting a performance review for an under- performing staff member. In order to maximize the staff member correcting their behavior, at the end of the meeting you should:
    d) have the staff member say exactly what actions he or she wants to take within an agreed timeline

11. In a presentation, which of the following statements would you not choose:
    a) I am not the expert in this area and would welcome your input

12. The six most fundamental principles of influence to be discovered by social psychological research are:
    c) commitment/consistency, authority, reciprocity, liking, social proof & scarcity.

Now update your Learning Journal (page 61)

6 Rules of Influence
Job Aid

Free Download

To download this job aid go to **www.tpc.net.au/tools**
and follow the online instructions.

METHODS OF PERSUASION

Part 4

#1 Aid to Persuasion: Proof & Logic

The ability to influence or persuade is an exercise in both proof and logic. Influencers must bring together various facts, insights, and values that others share or can be persuaded to accept (proof), and then show that these ideas lead more or less plausibly to a conclusion (logic).

Persuasion itself is an attempt to demonstrate the truth of an assertion or set of assertions to shape a logical argument. However arguments can be valid or invalid. A valid argument should be compelling in the sense that it is capable of convincing someone about the truth of a conclusion. However, this depends more on the skill of the person constructing the argument to manipulate the person who is being convinced.

In any persuasive dialogue the rules of interaction are either negotiated by the parties involved or determined by social norms. Ideally the goal of persuasive dialogue is for participants to arrive jointly at a conclusion by mutually accepted inferences.

Influence protocol

There are various stages which take place in any persuasive dialogue. These stages can be regarded as 'influence protocol' and include:

1. **Presentation: Raising awareness of the problem, by posing a question, debating an issue or voicing disagreement.**

2. **Opening: Agreement on rules such as how evidence is to be presented, how facts will be sourced, how different interpretations will be handled.**

3. **Persuasion: Application of logical principals according to the agreed-upon rules.**

4. **Closing: When termination conditions have been met. For example, a time limitation or the determination of an arbiter.**

"We perceive and are affected by changes too subtle to be described."

Henry David Thoreau (1817-1862)
American naturalist, poet and philosopher.

1

Complete Activity # 6
Power Word Match

"The question for each man is not what he would do if he had the means, time, influence, and educational advantages, but what he will do with the things he has."

Hamilton

Activity 6: Power Word Match

Circle the words below that would be considered Power Words. Once you have completed this activity, check back with the list provided in your Learning Short-take® Booklet. (Try not to look back before you have finished!)

1

Amazing

General

Outrageous

Last Chance

Mediocre

Superb

Satisfactory

Brilliant

Well known

First class

Non-customizable

You Have Won

Hurry

Standard

Unquestionable

Time is running out

Frequent

Generous

Tempting

Fascinating

Glorious

Abundant

Conclusion

Forced

Agenda

#2 Aid to Persuasion: Powerful Words

Words to use with

1

Communication in General

Outrageous	Dazzling	Splendid
Magnificent	Petite	Ample
Fascinating	Eccentric	Glorious
Amazing	Phenomenal	Lively
Tempting	Tremendous	Brilliant
Tranquil	Appealing	Worthwhile
Incredible	Gorgeous	Abundant
Gigantic	Comfortable	Marvelous
Generous	Tantalizing	Exuberant
Memorable	Spectacular	Superb
Vivid	Quaint	Stunning
First class	Exceptional	Breathtaking
Quintessential	Unquestionable	

Sales Communication

Free	Personal	Save now
Open at once	Immediate	Improved
Save	Sale	More #1 choice
Time is running out	You Have Won	New
Reserved	Big	Values
Updated	Hurry	Last Chance
Everyone is…	Urgent	You don't want to miss out

Now update your Learning Journal (page 61)

44

#3 Aid to Persuasion: Body Language

What happens at the body level influences the mind. What happens with the mind helps mold the body. How does the body influence the mind?

When you pay attention to how your emotions are embodied in your body language, it helps you tap into your emotional intelligence - the deeper inner resources that go beyond words.

In other words: you can be both more authentic and more effective, at work and in your relationships.

As humans we can modify our gestures consciously, making voluntary movements as well as displaying unconscious breathing shifts, skin tone changes and micro-muscle movements.

We use our bodies to convey interest or disinterest, to establish rapport with others, or to stop them in their tracks. We learn cultural norms about appropriate body language from people of any gender, age and status in our daily lives and can sometimes discover how our habitual presentations can elicit markedly different responses in other parts of the world.

1

"Body language communicates something whether we wish to communicate or not."

Jules Collingwood

We can use other people's body language to help us create rapport with them and persuade them to make a particular decision or take a course of action. If we place our attention on the other person or group of people, open our peripheral vision and quieten our internal comments we will notice the rhythm of their whole body movements, speech and gestures. If we then match these rhythms with our own bodies we will find ourselves being included.

This is not the same as deliberate mimicking. The intent is to match the rhythm without attracting conscious attention to it.

When we feel engaged by the other person we can test the level of rapport by doing something discreetly different and noticing whether the other person changes what they are doing in response. If they do, you can lead them into a different rhythm or influence the discussion more easily.

In larger groups it is important to observe group dynamics and identify the peer group leaders. These will be the people with others around them, the one's whose movements will be slightly ahead of the others and change first. If we want to influence the whole group, these are the people to match. This can be achieved by establishing rapport with each group leader individually or simultaneously if we are within their visual field. It is possible to change the direction of quite a large gathering by these techniques.

#4 Aid to Persuasion: Presentation Skill

Truly excellent influencing skills require a healthy combination of interpersonal, communication, presentation and assertiveness techniques. It is about adapting and modifying your personal style when you become aware of the affect you are having on other people, while still being true to yourself. Behavior and attitude change are what's important, not changing who you are or how you feel and think.

Influence is about understanding yourself and the impact you have on others. You could be doing the most brilliant presentation you have ever created, however if you have not brought your audience with you, the brilliance is wasted.

"Of the modes of persuasion furnished by the spoken word there are three kinds.
The first kind depends on the personal character of the speaker;
the second on putting the audience into a certain frame of mind;
the third on the proof, provided by the words of the speech itself."

Aristotle

Presenting a persuasive argument

In presenting any persuasive argument, whether to an audience of one or to many, consider the following:

- Know your audience.
- Pitch your message appropriately.
- Plan your material according to the relevant information needs of attendees.
- Develop persuasive communication messages.
- Practice - fine tune your presentation style to better inform, influence and convince.

"It doesn't matter what's going on internally for you - if it isn't perceived by the other person, then it doesn't exist, other than in your mind."

Impact Factory

Complete Activity # 7
Presentation Case Study

Activity 7: Presentation Case Study

Reflect on a presentation that you have given at work recently. You may choose a formal business presentation that you prepared and presented to a large group, or an informal presentation that was more ad hoc, say, at a smaller team meeting.

Without consideration for content of this Learning Short-take®, complete the following table in as much detail as possible:

What was the presentation?	What went well during the presentation?	What could have gone better?

Activity 7: Continued

Reflect on your key learnings so far as a result of this Learning Short-take®. Focus as well specifically on Part 4 - Methods of Persuasion.

What would you add now to this presentation, if you could deliver the same presentation again?	What would be the benefit?

Now, think of a future presentation that you either have scheduled, or know may be possible.

What general things will you add to your presentation in order to maximize your influence?

Now update your Learning Journal (page 61)

50

THE CHALLENGES OF INFLUENCE

Part 5

Influencing Change: The Challenges

There are many factors or levers to influencing change, but one of the key ones is that 'people don't resist change, they resist being changed.'

If we want to help people change, we have to help them decide the change is in their best interest. We have to influence them, not force change upon them.

Here are five things you can do, starting right now, to influence change in others:

1 - "Get" their perspective

Your perspective, goals and belief in the change don't really matter. All that matters is the perspective and beliefs of the other person. We must start by understanding their view of the world, their concerns, fears and assumptions regarding the change. Doing this will definitely help you counter some of these concerns. However, the real benefit in truly understanding their perspective is that you are valuing their opinion and they will feel they are a part of a conversation, not a sales pitch.

> Be it true or false, what is said about a person often has as much influence on their lives, and especially on their destinies, as what they do.
>
> Victor Hugo

2 - Acknowledge their perspective

You may not agree with their assumptions or share their fears and concerns, but you can acknowledge how they feel. Let them know that you understand their point of view and that it is a valid view. Part of the reason people resist being changed is that they never feel validated or acknowledged. Forgo this step at your peril.

3 - Speak to their interests

Once you know more about their issues and concerns you can help them see a different perspective. By acknowledging their perspective as a valid one, their mind will likely be more open to hearing a new perspective. Talk to them about the differences in your perspectives. Reduce their fears. Build a clearer picture of the future after the change, explaining the parts of it that will be of greatest interest and benefit in their mind.

4 - Recognize natural tendencies

Everyone has their own natural tendencies towards change. Some are more open and move more quickly to a new approach or system. Others are more cautious. If you often find yourself as the influencer of change, perhaps you are in the later group. Be aware that not everyone will move at the same rate.

5 - Be patient

Give people some time. Let them reflect on what you have shared with them. Give them time to justify a new position in their mind. Recognize that by giving people time it may also help them 'save face' as they begin to advocate a change that they had previously opposed.

In summary

With these five approaches you give yourself a better chance to influence others to change. Each of these alone will help you but taken together they greatly reduce resistance and help others move towards a changed perspective and actions. At a minimum you will have reduced people's resistance to change. At best they won't feel they are being changed they will recognize the change as their own.

10 ethical influence strategies

There are ten ethical influence strategies useful in a changing environment:

1. Legitimizing - referring to or using recognized authority.
2. Logical Persuading - using logic to persuade the person.
3. Appealing to Friendship - asking friends for favors or assistance.
4. Socializing - establishing rapport to find commonalities and to build a connection.
5. Consulting - presenting a problem and asking for input.
6. Stating - boldly and directly stating what you want, believe, or need.
7. Appealing to Values - inspiring cooperation by appealing to values, emotions, or feelings.
8. Modeling - setting an example for others to follow.
9. Exchanging - giving something of value to the person in return for something you want.
10. Alliance Building - building an alliance of supporters who can help you influence others.

 Complete Activity # 8
Planning to Influence

Activity 8: Planning to Influence

Identify a current situation or opportunity where you need to influence another party or parties. Complete the following table.

Describe the influence situation	
What is the other party's perspective on this situation (their view)?	
How will you acknowledge their perspective when preparing your for your dialogue or presentation?	
What are the other party's interests in this situation?	
How will you speak to these interests in preparing your dialogue or presentation?	

Now update your Learning Journal (page 61)

"Every life is a profession of faith, and exercises an inevitable and silent influence."

Henri Frédéric Amiel (1821-1881), Swiss writer

tpc★

BUILDING A LIFE
OF INFLUENCE

Part 6

Other Ways to create an Influential Life

With it's origin in George Orwell's book 1984, this mathematical equation is often used by motivational speakers as a way of teaching synergy and that the whole is greater than the sum of it's parts.

Express an original idea, or a common one in an insightful new way

Consider how likely it would be for the newspapers to publish a story about a person learning 2 + 2 = 4. Compare that to a revolutionary physical proof as to why 2 + 2 actually equalled 5. Of course, anyone can make the claim, but if it is substantiated by something others haven't considered, the likelihood of getting people's attention is greatly increased.

Meet and speak to more people

Making business connections and having a strong network of people with whom you can discuss and share ideas is very beneficial. Start with organizations to which you're already connected. Join your college alumni club, appropriate professional organization if there's a chapter in your city, and get involved in a special interest group.

The Internet offers plenty of ways to meet people and develop friendships, and given the trends on the internet, friends of friends grow networks easily. Forums are an easy, fun way to do this, although often time-consuming. A forum basically has users with common interests post subjects like they would do on a noticeboard, to which others can post replies. Forums exist for virtually everything/anything from music, to politics, to blogging. Other options are newsgroups, chat rooms, and other interactive websites.

Raise issues/opinions ignored by others

In business, it's easy to keep under the radar of opinion. Consider issues that are yet to be discussed in meetings. Having opinions that are different to others and having the courage to express them, may result in a greater degree of influence.

Volunteer with a group

People who work for free means they are passionate and it also opens doors. Consider a person volunteering on the campaign of an important Minister. Chances are that the person would never have had the person's ear if he hadn't offered to help. Organizations can always use another hand to do chores they don't care to do, but if someone is volunteering for those things, the organizations are likely to be indulgent, and help them with their resources in return.

Complete Activity # 9
Creating an Influential Life

Activity 9: Creating an Influential Life

1 Consider three strategies that you could undertake right now to create a more influential life. Record these strategies in the table below.

Influence Strategy	How I will use this in my life right now
1.	
2.	
3.	

Now update your Learning Journal (page 61)

Section 2

LEARNING JOURNAL

The Learning Journal is used throughout the Learning Short-take® process to record your key learnings, hot tips and things to remember.

Update your Learning Journal at anytime throughout the Learning Short-take® process. Ensure you complete your Learning Journal after you finish each activity. Then turn back to the Participant Guide to continue your learning.

Learning Journal

As you work through this Learning Short-take®, make detailed notes on this page of the lessons you have learned and any useful skill areas. For each lesson or refresher point think about how you could further develop this skill. Your coach will want to discuss these with you in your Skill Development Action Planning meeting.

2

"…that is what learning is.
You suddenly understand something you've understood all your life, but in a new way."

Doris Lessing

"Act as though it were impossible to fail. "

Winston Churchill

"The wise do at once what the fool does later."
Baltasar Gracian (1601-58), Spanish Jesuit priest and author.

Learning or Idea	Action to be taken	Result Expected

2

Learning Journal - continued

Learning or Idea	Action to be taken	Result Expected

"Anyone who stops learning is old, whether at twenty or eighty."
Henry Ford

Learning or Idea	Action to be taken	Result Expected

2

"Setting an example is not the main means of influencing another, it is the only means."

Albert Einstein

Section 3

SKILL DEVELOPMENT ACTION PLAN

Your Skill Development Action Plan is the last Step in the Learning Short-take® process. After you have completed the Participant Guide and all Activities update your Learning Journal then complete this section.

Skill Development Action Plan

This is the most important part of the program - your individual Skill Development Action Plan.

You need to complete this plan before meeting with your manager or prior to on-going coaching. You will discuss it in detail with your manager or coach as he or she will ensure that you have everything you need to complete the tasks and activities.

Once you have completed your **Skill Development Action Plan** schedule a meeting time with your manager or coach to review your plan. Take your participant guide and all other documentation received during the training course to this meeting.

Remember - you have committed to your **Skill Development Action Plan**, and need to make time to complete your tasks!

"The mind, once stretched by a new idea, never regains its original dimensions."

Oliver Wendell Holmes

"Whatever you can do or dream you can - begin it. Boldness has genius, power and magic."

Johann Wolfgang von Goethe

"Imagination is the eye of the soul."
Joseph Joubert (1754-1824)

Task or activity (Be specific)	Measure (this will help you to know you have achieved it)	Date (Be specific)
Reflect on your Learning Journal. Transfer action items that you can apply to your job. Ensure that you include some 'stretch goals' and also a blend of short, medium and long term goals.	Apart from you, who else is needed to assist you in achieving your goal.	Be specific. A general date such as 'Quarter 1', 'August', or 'by end of year' is vague and more likely to result in not achieving your target. Be specific – e.g. 22nd November.

Ideas for discussion with my manager

Ideas

3

Congratulations!

You've now completed this Learning Short-take®.

Meet with your Manager/Coach to discuss your
Skill Development Action Plan.

"When we are no longer able
to change a situation, we are
challenged to change ourselves."

Victor Frankl

extra

QUICK REFERENCE

This Quick Reference provides you with a summary of key concepts, models and reference material from Learning Short-takes®. We have also included some quotations to ponder.

Use this section as a quick reference to keep your learning active.

4

Influence is about discovering the principles that determine beliefs, create attitudes, and move people to agreement and action. Influence examines the process that causes humans to change. When influence is used correctly, it efficiently moves people in positive directions.

 **" There are, then, these three means of effecting persuasion. The man who is to be in command of them must, it is clear, be able**

(1) to reason logically,

(2) to understand human character and goodness in their various forms, and

(3) to understand the emotions - that is, to name them and describe them, to know their causes and the way in which they are excited. "

Aristotle, Rhetoric I, ch. 2)

4

4

Social influence is when the actions or thoughts of individual(s) are changed by other individual(s).

Three Components of Social Influence

Conformity: A type of social influence in which individuals change their attitudes or behavior in order to *adhere to existing social norms.*

Compliance: A form of social influence involving *direct request* from one person to another.

Obedience: A form of social influence in which one person *obeys direct orders* from another to perform some action(s).

4

" I seek the serenity to accept what I cannot change; the courage to change what I can; and the wisdom to know the difference. "

Author unknown

Circle of Influence / Circle of Concern

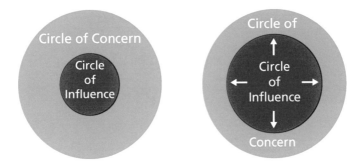

Accept the issues for which you have no control over, for now or forever. Proactively focus on **what you can do**. When you accept the things you can't immediately control, it frees you to focus on the things you can do something about.

4

" No star ever rose or set without influence somewhere. "

Lord Edward Robert Bulwer Lytton
"Owen Meredith", Lucile (pt. II, canto VI)

Agents of Influence

The Bungler doesn't understand how to use influence and fumbles away opportunities for beneficial change.

The Smuggler understands how to use influence but does this dishonestly producing gain that is one-sided and temporary.

The Sleuth uncovers powerful principles in the influence situation and brings them to the surface to the long-term advantage of both parties.

Six Rules of Influence

4

1 - Rule of Reciprocity
A person tries to repay, in kind, what another person has provided.

2 - Commitment and Consistency
The desire to look consistent within words, beliefs, attitudes and deeds.

3 - Social Proof
Determining what is correct by finding out what other people think is correct

4 - Liking
People prefer to say yes to individuals they know and like.

5 - Authority
Compliance with the requests of an authority

6 - Scarcity
People assign more value to opportunities when they are less available.

Methods of Persuasion

4

#1: Proof & Logic

#2: Powerful Words

#3: Body Language

#4: Presentation Skill

4

❝ Body language communicates something whether we wish to communicate or not. ❞

Jules Collingwood

" Of the modes of persuasion furnished by the spoken word there are three kinds.

The first kind depends on the personal character of the speaker;

the second on putting the audience into a certain frame of mind;

the third on the proof, provided by the words of the speech itself. "

Aristotle

4

**" A teacher
affects eternity;
he can never tell where
his influence stops. "**

Henry Brooks Adams

❝ Be it true or false,
what is said about a person
often has as much
influence on their lives,
and especially on their
destinies, as what they do. ❞

Victor Hugo

4

ff You can exert no influence if you are not susceptible to influence. JJ

Carl Jung

NEXT STEPS

Congratulations! You have now completed this Learning Short-take® title. The entire list of Learning Short-takes® can be found on the TPC website.

In this section we have suggested Learning Short-take® titles for you that will build your learning. You may order these Learning Short-takes® online at www.tpc.net.au or from your bookstores.

Persuasive Presentation Skills
Create, Prepare and Design with Confidence

Learning Short-take® Outline

Persuasive Presentation Skills combines self-study with realistic workplace activities to provide presenters with the key skills and techniques to prepare and deliver dynamic presentations. After assessing your current approach to preparing and delivering presentations, **Persuasive Presentation Skills** will help you develop unique and innovative strategies to improve your presentation success from small meetings to large audiences. You will learn to effectively plan your communication by using a real-life upcoming presentation.

A dynamic and powerful presentation gives you a platform to communicate your message effectively, influence your audience and spark desired action. Effective presenters spend a considerable amount of time preparing for their presentation, ensuring that the structure, content and communication style is appropriate for their audience. It is often what happens before the presenter enters the room that dictates the success of the presentation.

Persuasive Presentation Skills includes the **Persuasive Presentation Skills Presentation Planner**, provided as a free downloadable tool.

Learning Objectives

- Explain the importance of preparation in delivering a successful presentation.
- Explain how to structure your presentation to deliver key messages.
- Describe how to connect with your audience and maintain attention.
- Identify key factors for enhancing your message and projecting credibility.
- How to design and use visual aids to support your message.
- Describe how to control your nervous energy.
- Create a Skill Development Action Plan.

5

Course Content

- Part 1: Preparation Fundamentals
- Part 2: Presentation Structure
- Part 3: Connecting with Your Audience
- Part 4: Developing an Individual Presentation Style
- Part 5: Tips and Tricks for Getting Your Message Across
- Part 6: Creating Effective Support Materials
- Part 7: Mastering Nervous Energy

Negotiating for Success
The Process and Tools for Win/Win

Course Content

- Part 1: Negotiation Defined
- Part 2: Preparing for Negotiation
- Part 3: The Negotiation Process
- Part 4: Interests
- Part 5: Inventing Options for Mutual Gain
- Part 6: Standards
- Part 7: People
- Part 8: BATNA
- Part 9: Close

Learning Short-take® Outline

Negotiating for Success combines self-study with realistic workplace activities to develop skills in successful negotiating. This Learning Short-take® is particularly relevant to those who are new to negotiating or who would benefit from strengthening negotiation skills. You will learn how to effectively prepare for a negotiation using your own real life business opportunity and how to incorporate key steps and elements into the negotiation process. You will identify how to achieve a win/win outcome in a negotiation and will be able to differentiate positional bargaining from principled negotiation.

Negotiation is an ever-present feature of both our personal and professional lives, and in the business world effective negotiators are in high demand. Bringing a complex negotiation to a successful conclusion can be one of the most individually exhilarating and valuable aspects of business today.

Negotiating for Success includes the **Negotiation Planner**, provided as a free downloadable tool.

Learning Objectives

- Define negotiation - what it is and what it isn't.
- Explain the win/win model of negotiation.
- Differentiate between positional bargaining and principled negotiation.
- List the steps in preparing for a negotiation.
- Identify and explain the steps in the negotiation process.
- Define BATNA.
- Create a Skill Development Action Plan.

Listen and Be Listened To
Get Inside the Customer's Mind

Learning Short-take® Outline

combines self-study with realistic workplace activities to provide you with the key skills and techniques of effective and enhanced listening. You will learn to build more effective work relationships with your co-workers and leaders by tuning into key communication messages and responding appropriately. You will learn tips, tricks and techniques to boost active listening capability and discover that effective listening helps command respect from both the speakers and listeners point of view.

Our unique view of the world and personal style - based on our values, beliefs, attitudes and behaviors - affects how we act, perceive information, and communicate with others. It also influences the way we listen and how others listen to us. When we expect to hear certain things, we may pay attention to only what interests us. Our perception about a person, situation or subject influences our reception of information, and how much attention we choose to pay. **Listen and Be Listened To** breaks down the art and skill of active listening which is critical to building and maintaining effective working relationships.

Listen and Be Listened To includes an impactful **'Listening Tips' Wall Chart**, provided to you as a free download.

Learning Objectives

- Define listening.
- Explain why listening is important.
- Identify the barriers to effective listening.
- Identify their listening style and the listening style of others.
- Demonstrate techniques for active listening.
- Create a Skill Development Action Plan.

Course Content

- Part 1: Listening & Communication

- Part 2: Listening versus Hearing

- Part 3: Barriers to Effective Listening

- Part 4: Your Natural Listening Style

- Part 5: Passive Listening

- Part 6: Active Listening

- Part 7: Better Questions, Better Answers